Justice For All

The Search for a Theology of Biblical Justice in
Light of the Three Angels' Messages of
Revelation

Lemuel Valendez Sapian

JUSTICE FOR ALL : The Search for a Theology of Biblical
Justice in Light of the Three Angels' Messages of
Revelation

For information contact :

Brimingstone Press

www.brimingstone.press

Book and Cover design by Lemuel Sapian
ISBN: 978-1-953562-03-6
Second Edition: October 2021

10 9 8 7 6 5 4 3 2 1

Table of Contents

"The Lord Jesus demands our acknowledgment of the rights of every man. Men's social rights, and their rights as Christians, are to be taken into consideration. All are to be treated with refinement and delicacy, as the sons and daughters of God."

- Ellen G. White, *Gospel Workers*, pg. 123.

Foreword

Of the Seven Churches in the book of Revelation, the church of Philadelphia, known as "brotherly love," wasone of two churches not given a rebuke from Jesus. As students of prophecy, we know that this phase of church history fell between 1833 and 1844, where the seeds of Adventism began to coalesce and come together during the Second Great Awakening via the Millerite Movement. It is during this time, thatthe faithful advocated strongly against the institution of slavery, and for moral, health, and temperance reform.

This phase of the church saw to the preparation for Christ's return in connection with actively using their platform to address the social injustices and moral depravity of that day. In this book, my friend and colleague Lemuel Sapian, boldly calls us to hearken back and to rekindle the spirit of the Philadelphia church.

With his use of powerful primary sources, and a writing style that makes the complex easy to understand, Brother Sapian calls us to navigate through these politically polarizing times, and to do what God calls us to do, to carve our own path with divinely inspired solutions to address the inequalities and injustices that this nation faces. It is a powerful appeal to minister like Jesus and reflect His character in these last days.

PETER K. CHUNG

History Teacher and Evangelist for Revelation of Hope Ministries

Introduction

The Seventh-day Adventist Church has maintained its prophetic identity as the Remnant Church of Bible prophecy. Identifying with the Remnant of the pure woman depicted in Revelation, we have confidently preached and taught the Three Angels' Messages of Revelation 14 as our peculiar mission.

While we stress the importance and significance of preparing for the soon coming of Christ, there is considerable debate surrounding how the church at large should deal with temporal issues, especially in the area of societal justice.

Some believe we are to separate entirely from

temporal concerns, and disregard societal issues. Others believe we are to make an impact in the social scene to be more effective proclaimers of truth and to be more winsome. Many more are stuck in between, vacillating between the two positions, or vainly trying to find a middle ground.

It is the purpose of this book to explore the historical and *Inspired* evidence on this vital topic. I have endeavored to research, with much prayer, the issues which are relevant to today's society, and seek a Biblical solution to the question on how much involvement in them we should have as a people.

Much of the information included in this book had only surfaced as it was being researched. I pray that it was the work of the Holy Spirit, and that we as the Remnant of Bible prophecy awaken to these essential truths.

Prejudice cannot be mixed with godliness any more than iron can mix with clay. It is my hope that you will read this volume with an open mind.

I do not ask that you accept wholesale what is being taught within, only seek the leading of God's Spirit, and ask Him how we should handle these issues in society as we get closer and closer to the second Advent.

And let us treat each other with justice and fairness, and without any prejudice. As the Scriptures admonish,

> *"But if you show prejudice, you are commiting sin and are convicted by thelaw as violators."*

> \- James 2:9, NET

That we all reflect the character we will have in Heaven, that of our Lord Jesus Christ, is my prayer.

LEMUEL V. SAPIAN

Chapter One:

The Rights of Men

Incontrovertibly written in the Declaration of Independence of the United States of America is the idea that "all men are created equal, that they are endowed by their Creator with certain unalienable Rights, that among these are Life, Liberty and the Pursuit of Happiness." While Thomas Jefferson wrote these venerable words, it was Benjamin Franklin who suggested the preceding words be "We hold these truths to be self-evident..." and our Declaration of

Independence was born, declaring a government deriving its power from the consent of the governed, akey Enlightenment idea.

But it is the larger influence of Christianity that has established the rights of all, contrary to the reprehensible notions of many Americans who wish touse their religious and national identity to deprive the rights of their fellow humans. Christ declared, in Matthew 25:45 (KJV) -

> *"...Inasmuch as ye have done it untoone of the least of these my brethren, ye have done it unto me."*

How we treat the disadvantaged of the world is how we treat our Lord and Savior. The American founders implicitly realized this sacred notion and understood the value of liberating men to pursue happiness, one of the chief sources of which, is a knowledge of purpose and truth. It is also evident from a cursory reading of American history, that it is rife with moral shame. The treatment and military subjugation of native tribes, and of course, the moral stain of slavery and its subsequent continuation in the form of racial segregation and prejudice.

We, in the post-millennial era have found ways to dismiss our past history, assuring ourselves that a repeat will never happen. But there is a reason bitter history should never be forgotten. We pride ourselves as being the "greatest nation" on the face of the earth, and we would hardly object, but only as a means to remind ourselves to be eternally vigilant and cognizant of the inevitability of a return to medieval horrors and tyranny.

It is not that America is criminal; she is not perfect, but neither is any nation on this earth. Still, America is supposed to stand at the vanguard of religious freedom and social liberty and justice, even as these institutions are being threatened by the very people that swore to protect them. There has always been a vein of intolerance in the nation, against minority religions and systems of unbelief, against minority races, and against lifestyles many deem reprehensible. And there will always be a need for voices and pens of dissent against every form of bigotry and tyranny. Sure, even bigots have their rights, but the boundary is where they would infringe upon the rights of another. It is wishful thinking to apply the Biblical Golden Rule to civil law, since so many are driven by self-preservation and selfishness. But it is a principle we hold to those that claim to be Christians. There is no room for bigotry in the religion of Christ. And in the realm of the civil sphere, we expect the Constitution to safeguard our basic rights as humans, to maintain the order of providing each individual their liberty to be free of molestation by individuals or institutions.

As Christians, we must stand up for the rights of all, even those that do not agree with us. We were not called to be smug pharisees, jeering at the alleged spiritual inferiority of non-Christians. Many who do, "strain at a gnat, and swallow a camel" (Matthew 23:24 KJV).

As Christians, we hold no claim to superiority. Our only claim is to Jesus Christ, and Him crucified. And He died for all mankind, with no exception. Provision has been given for "whosoever will" to partake of the "water of life freely" (Revelation 22:17 KJV). There is no "limited atonement." Christ died for all, and only a rejection of His sacrifice will disqualify one from the Kingdom above.

Therefore, while we wait upon that Kingdom from above to arrive, we must practice Christian charity on this earth. Yes, we understand that the laws of earthly kingdoms must be allowed to maintain harmonious civil peace and order, but only as a temporal means and never to infringe upon the conscience or enforce one to conform to a religious culture that they have not accepted in their hearts.

This is why we need to safeguard the rights for all, both in the sight of Almighty God, and in sight of the American Constitution.

Chapter Two:
Church, State, and Civil
Rights

There are many in the religious world that rightfully see the concerns regarding mixing religion with the state. There are also many varying degrees of religious entanglement with the state. The most obvious and egregious examples are theocracies that have existed throughout history. In the Christian worldview, the ancient theocracy of Israel was ordained and led directly by God. However, down the line many other worldly kingdoms and empires would claim the mantle of being led by God in differing degrees.

Today, there aren't very many true theocracies, with the Vatican of Catholicism, Mount Athos of the Eastern Orthodox, and the Theocratic Islamic Republic of Iran being the most prominent. The more common modern examples of Church and State union are states with official, established religions, and those states that have religious beliefs enshrined in their constitutions. Then you have the lowest tier category with states that give constitutional freedom of religion, but prominently favor a majority religion.

As Seventh-day Adventists and citizens of the United States of America, we advocate for the full and complete separation of Church and State, as legally required by our national Constitution, under the Establishment Clause of its First Amendment. This means that no law legislated in the United States of America should favor an establishment of religion, no matter how prominent and traditional that religion may be. This is exemplified by Jefferson's "Wall of

Separation" quote and forms the basis of our understanding of the "separation of Church and State." This means the separation of the spheres of Caesar and of God Almighty, as indicated by Christ in Matthew 22:

> *18 But Jesus perceived their wickedness, and said, Why tempt ye me, ye hypocrites?*
>
> *19 Shew me the tribute money. And they brought unto him a penny.*
>
> *20 And he saith unto them, Whose is this image and superscription?*
>
> *21 They say unto him, Caesar's. Then saith he unto them, Render therefore unto Caesar the things which are Caesar's; and unto God the things that are God's.*
>
> *22 When they had heard these*

words, they marvelled, and left
him, and went their way.

Here Christ establishes a principle simple to understand. There are things in the temporal world that are under the purview of Caesar, for which God allowed a certain level of governance, it is apart from the greater reign of God. Christ's response to the Pharisees, who took along with them "Herodians" (v. 16) who were representatives of King Herod, the vassal King of Judea, confounded them and they "marveled."

Christ was conveying the fact that the secular state could not in any way reflect the government of God, except in the case of establishing order as peaceable relations between men. This is what we need to keep in mind while reading Paul's admonition regarding "powers that be" in Romans chapter 13. The government of Christ's and Paul's day was the Pagan Roman Empire, a secular state with Pagan religious trappings that persecuted Christians.

Yet, Christians were admonished to be obedient

to such powers in their spheres because the "powers that be" were agents of God, not to enforce the standards of His Kingdom, but to enforce the standards of a temporal, worldly state, to keep the civil peace. In this American Republic, keeping the civil peace means to be inclusive of many diverse beliefs and cultures, since America is a melting pot of backgrounds and races. We are to uphold and defend the rights of all, even those whose worldview we do not accept.

The Roman Empire of Christ's day was a similar melting pot of cultures. As an empire that ruled the known world at that time, Imperial Rome oversaw swathes of land that had many tribes, languages and cultures. Christ did not attempt to gain worldly political power over Roman emperors; He was content to extend the principles of His kingdom into every heart. Christ was no worldly religious activist in the sense that He attempted to enforce the laws of God's Heavenly Kingdom upon a worldly and temporal state.

He made it clear that His kingdom was "not of this world" (John 18:36).

Yet Christ was a civil activist in the sense that He enjoined obedience to earthly authority in its proper sphere, and commanded men to love their neighbors as themselves. In other words, Jesus knew and wanted to impart the basic truth to His followers that while worldly kingdoms cannot hope to reflect the Kingdom of God, they can become paragons of civil virtue and tolerance, rightfully rendering unto Caesar that which is Caesar's, and to God, that which is God's.

I firmly believe that at its inception, the United States of America has reflected this basic concept in its Constitution. By separating Church and State by its inclusion of the Establishment and Free Exercise clauses in its First Amendment, the Constitution gives every person within the borders of this nation the freedom to exercise their belief in a religion of their choice, or to choose no religion at all. This legal protection should ensure that no one is molested by law for their religious beliefs or unbelief. To wit, no one should be forced by law to abide by any religious-based observance or statute.

This makes America the first in the history of the world, to successfully and legally separate Church and State completely, and put an end to the religious wars that plagued Europe for centuries. In conjunction with the Enlightenment ideology of government exercising powers by the consent of the governed, the Protestant principle of Church and State separation is the closest to the Biblical New Covenant model of civil governance. Unfortunately, this principle has been under attack by what we would term "Christian Civil Moralists."

Thus defined: A "Christian Civil Moralist" is a proponent of Christian "civil religion" where the civil moral code is to reflect a particular religion's moral ethics and standards, usually at the mutual exclusion of other systems of religious belief and non-belief. Civil religion is precisely what the First Amendment to the US Constitution was trying to avoid. Cognizant of the fact that America was and will be a melting pot of many cultures and beliefs, the American Founders knew the only way to keep the civil peace was to enact legal toleration for all religions. Violating the Establishment or Free Exercise clauses would cause excluded religious groups to become disfranchised and eventually persecuted. This is why there needs to be a "wall" of separation between Church and State.

What about civil activism in contrast to the religious-based activism we just defined above? I believe this is within the duties of a Christian to fulfill. Calling for justice in society and fairness, along with protesting the mistreatment of "the least of these," do not contradict the principles of Christ. To treat others as we would like to be treated is a basic Christian principle, and as Christ died for all, including those who didn't believe in Him, we are to be active in making sure others have their basic rights preserved even if they don't believe, look, or speak the same way we do.

To conclude this chapter, we find that there is a difference between religious and civil activism when it comes to temporal matters. To campaign for the Kingdom of God we appeal to the hearts of men, not to Capitol Hill. However, to secure the rights of all to liberty and justice, we have a duty to treat our follow man as we would like to be treated. We will discuss this further in Chapter Nine: The Solution.

We cannot stand silently by as prejudice and bigotry has the potential to sweep through the land. While slavery as an institution was dealt with in the 19th century, racial and economic prejudice has continued to prevail in some form. We must continue to preach against the sins of injustice, then admonish the wayward to look to Christ and His coming Kingdom where there is no prejudice and intolerance in any form, except the intolerance of evil and sin.

Chapter Three:
The Rights of One Are the Rights of All

It is often asked whether the protection of rights other than our own should be the concern of a Christian. It is distressing to see Christian political activism largely concerned only about Christians. Take the movement to "restore" prayer in public schools. State sponsored prayer in public school has been prohibited since *Engel v. Vitale* (1962), and this decision has been upheld since. However, most conservative Christians that you talk to today would balk at the suggestion that a Muslim or Hindu prayer should be sponsored by the public school system. So, what they are essentially saying is that they want prayer "restored" in schools, but only Christian, or at least Judeo-Christian prayers.

While as Christians we would desire that all men and women would pray to the true God through Christ, we should realize that not every individual believes this way. Forcing them by legal edict to pray or worship a God they don't believe in is not making them Christians, it's making them hypocrites. Instead, we should respect the rights of all to choose and practice their religion and beliefs or unbelief. By doing so, we become a powerful witness through our character.

If we do this, Christianity will no longer be looked upon as an exacting, power hungry, forceful, and political religion. Rather, it will be a religion drawing people through the calling of the Holy Spirit. As the Lord explained to Zerubbabel:

"Not by might, nor by power,

but by my spirit, saith the Lord of hosts."

- Zechariah 4:6 KJV

Turning to temporal political machinery to uphold our religion only reveals that it is impotent. But even more than that, it shows to others we have little concern for anything else or anyone except ourselves, which is a very selfish approach and tends to repel people from, and not draw people to, our faith. That is why the approach of Christ is so very crucial a solution to today's cultural issues.

In Christ's day, the Samaritans were looked down upon as spiritual inferiors; they were marginalized minorities in Judea, blamed for national woes and misfortunes. They were considered racially inferior because of their assimilation and integration into Assyrian culture, spiritually inferior because their kingdom was the first to fall into apostasy and ruin and had lost their cultural identity.

Because Christ taught cultural, political and

spiritual equality for Samaritans, the marginalized and rejected of Jewish society, He was even accused of being a Samaritan Himself. Not only that, but the Jews also suspected Him of also having a devil in Him.

> *"Then answered the Jews, and said unto him, Say we not well that thou art a Samaritan, and hast a devil?"*

- John 8:48 KJV

Often times when you stand up for the rights of minorities and other faiths, you will be accused of being one of them (in an attempt to disparage you and them) and of being on the devil's side. Don't let this tactic perplex you. It certainly didn't worry Christ!

When Christ sat and ate with the downtrodden of society and spoke to sinners, He did not endorse and participate in any unholy or sinful practice. Yet His life reveals a lot about what the Christian's role in today's society should be; aloof from politics but not aloof from the woes of men, refusing to condemn the powers that be, yet speaking for the downtrodden and less fortunate of the world, pointing out the sins of injustice but not attacking institutions. By revealing that even a lowly Samaritan was the neighbor of the vaunted and "favored" Jew, Christ demolished religious, racial and social bigotry and prejudice in one parable.

Therefore, we ask, is it our duty to stand up for the rights of all? Most certainly. Christians follow in the example of Christ, and since Christ defended the right of the spiritually and racially "inferior" Samaritan to be called a neighbor, and the duty of true believers to love him as oneself, we are to do the same for our fellow neighbors in our society today. They deserve the dignity and respect as fellow humans, whether or not they share the same skin color, religious belief, language, or economic status as we do. This is the way of Christ.

> *40 And the King shall answer and say unto them, Verily I say unto you, Inasmuch as ye have*

done it unto one of the least of these my brethren, ye have done it unto me.

41 Then shall he say also unto them on the left hand, Depart from me, ye cursed, into everlasting fire, prepared for the devil and his angels:

42 For I was an hungered, and ye gave me no meat: I was thirsty, and ye gave me no drink:

43 I was a stranger, and ye took me not in: naked, and ye clothed me not: sick, and in prison, and ye visited me not.

44 Then shall they also answer him, saying, Lord, when saw we thee an hungered, or athirst, or a stranger, or naked, or sick, or in prison, and did not minister unto thee?

45 Then shall he answer them, saying, Verily I say unto you, Inasmuch as ye did it not to one of the least of these, ye did it not to me.

46 And these shall go away into everlasting punishment: but the righteous into life eternal.

- Matthew 25 (KJV)

It is often tempting in our culture to marginalize and disfranchise those of minority status. But remember that part of our Christian duty is to treat others how we would like to be treated, and to love those not just of our own "tribe."

46 For if ye love them which love you, what reward have ye? do not even the publicans the same?

47 And if ye salute your brethren only, what do ye more than others? do not even the publicans so?

- Matthew 5 (KJV)

Does this mean we are to love the Muslim, the Hindu, or even the Satanist? Of course. We are not to love only those that love us.

Does this mean to love whites, blacks, browns, and any shade of skin and race not of our own? Of course.

Does this mean to love the homeless man on the street, despite some blaming his laziness for producing his predicament, or the rich oligarch who some believe is using his wealth to depopulate the earth (this is a strange narrative, but some believe it)? Regardless of what narrative you choose to believe, your Christian duty commands you to love them as you love yourself.

There is no room in true Christianity for bigotry of any sort. There is no room for narcissists or prejudice of any kind. Although even bigots and narcissists we are to love. We don't have to love what they do; in fact, we are to hate the sin and love the sinner. But we are also to protest with voice and pen the injustices perpetrated by tyrants, high and low, calling sin by its right name.

The Adventist flagship journal for Religious Liberty, *The American Sentinel,* once published this sobering thought by W. A. Blakely:

> *"...we must remember that if we would maintain our free institutions, we must protect the rights of minorities, and insure to them every privilege and immunity that is accorded the majority, and that every man's rights must be protected whether he stands alone or with the Nation. We must remember, too, the tendency of mankind to enforce upon others their opinions and their customs."*

- *The American Sentinel,* Vol. 6, No 6, February5, 1891

By treating others as we would like to be treated, we are living the character of Jesus.

Chapter Four:
The Remnant's Involvement in Calling for Justice in Society

At the turn of the 20th century, there were social upheavals that caused conflict in American society. It had been almost a half-century since slavery was abolished, and blacks were still having issues integrating into society. This was true not just in the racist South, but also in the North. It is now the 21st century, and still, we are seeing examples of discrimination and racism in today's America.

Seventh-day Adventism had separated itself from the mainstream Protestant world not only by its doctrines, such as embracing the seventh-day Sabbath, among other unique theological traits, but also through its insistence on Church and State separation. The Church also advocates for the religious liberty of all, not just their own.

Through its official Religious Liberty publication, *The American Sentinel*, also known as *The Sentinel of Liberty*, the Seventh-day Adventist Church continued to advocate Church and State separation. However, the *Sentinel's* work was not only in keeping intact the constitutional right of freedom of conscience, it also saw to the work of maintaining civil rights and social equality.

The *Sentinel* also saw the proper sphere in which conscientious Christians must operate with a civil voice. When the American imperial machine began to involve itself in expeditionary conflicts, especially in the conquest of the Philippines in the Spanish- American War at the turn of the 20th century, the indomitable Adventists protested in print, decrying the imperialist endeavor. The *Sentinel* also decried the brutality which the police visited upon many blacks.

Alonzo T. Jones made clear the *Sentinel's* position wasnot anarchist:

> *"THE AMERICAN SENTINEL does not believe in anarchy. It is a patriotic and religious duty to yield cheerful obedience to civil rulers in civil things."*

But he continues as to the proper function of civil government,

> *"By the very act of making men socialbeings, mutually dependent upon one another, and under mutual obligations each to respect the equal rights of the other, God ordained civil government, that the weak might be protected against the aggressions of the strong, that*

unlawful greed and oppression might be restrained, and that civilorder might be maintained."

- Alonzo T. Jones, *The American Sentinel*, Vol. 7, No. 35, September 8, 1892.

In this, Seventh-day Adventists remained in the minority within the Christian world. Often derided as siding with infidels, the *Sentinel* nonetheless continued its work in maintaining the distance between Church and State, as well as calling for the equal rights of all.

But the fight against oppression has always been met with hostility by many in America, even within the Adventist Church. Minorities are still discriminated against. Perhaps not as blatantly as during Jim Crow, but old habits die hard.

America has been beset by protests against social injustice to this day. Has it been any different from times past? The same spirit of oppression still reigns, even in modern America. We can never encourage lawlessness or condone violence. Yet the acts of brutality and oppression by authorities frustrate a people that will know no other way to react.

Calvin P. Bollman, writing for the *Sentinel* on August 30, 1900, addressed events of unrest at that time which was wreaking havoc in Mansfield, Ohio and New York City. It is interesting also that this astute Adventist writer differentiated between two types of "anarchists"– one which gave an *outward* profession for "law and order," and those that were outwardly subversive and destructive.

> *"The most dangerous anarchists are not those who commit overt acts of violence, but those who in the name of law and order override natural and constitutional rights. The 'red' anarchist, the anarchist who uses bomb, pistol, or stiletto, is less dangerous because his methods startle people and make them realize more fully than before the really beneficent*

character of whole-some laws honestly administered. The anarchist who, while professing great loyalty to law, overrides the principles of justice, is the more dangerous because he is more respectable, his methods less startling, and his work more lasting and vastly more far-reaching."

- Calvin P. Bollman, *The Sentinel of Liberty*, Vol. 15, No. 34, August 30, 1900.

Instead of condemning only the anarchist who opposed law by taking to the streets and destroying buildings and property, the Adventist writer brought attention to the "law and order" anarchist, one who professed loyalty to "law and order" but in actuality sought to subvert the constitutional rights of the individuals they were seeking to oppress.

Bollman critiqued the notion that law enforcement should always have immunity, since no lawman is above the law. Even God Himself will not abrogate His immutable law, and Christ kept every tittle of it.

Bollman brought to light two examples of the anarchist behavior of lawmen, each of which can be related to by people on either side of the political spectrum. The instance in Mansfield, OH was of a religious sect that taught divine healing.

When a member refused to be attended to by a medical professional and instead relied on the so-called healing abilities of the church, she and her newborn died. The distraught family blamed the misadventure on the sect and gathered a mob to manhandle and chase the sect members out of town.

Their free exercise forcibly removed from them, the sect members sought to meet in secret but were found out. The mob then began to harass them, and the local sheriff and his deputies joined the mob in chasing the sect members out of town on threat of physical force. The lawmen were violating the sect's constitutional rights of free religious exercise, and worse, did so under the auspices of their office.

The second incident of anarchy happened in New York City when a black burglar shot and killed a policeman. But it wasn't that event that Bollman referred to as anarchist; it was what happened afterwards that he termed *true* anarchy. First, he made it clear that there were also many white burglars who shot officers. Yet what occurred afterward was truly deplorable. Referencing the *Daily Chronicle*, Bollman quotes,

> "Investigation fully proves that the recent collision between whites and blacks in New York City was a police orgy. The negro who killed the white policeman could not have escaped justice if testimony showed that he deserved punishment. If the scales veered either way in such a case the accused was not likely to be the beneficiary. There was, therefore, not even the pretext

of miscarriage of justice to condone the merciless fury with which the real or apparent crime of the negro was revenged upon hundreds of innocent colored women and children. The helpless, the industrious, the sober, were maltreated. All law was violated by the brutal club swingers and pistol flourishers on the blacks. Race conflict is at least intelligible below Mason and Dixon's line. North of it it is also intelligible. In the South its causes are historic. In the North its cause is the license a brutal policeman feels to use his club or revolver independently of constitutional restraints. It is not merely race hatred that inspires him, it is a wantonness in the use of power."

- *Ibid.*

Appalled by this report, Bollman wrote,

> "So far as being a menace to popular government is concerned, the officers who upon an occasion of this kind makes common cause with the mob, is many fold more dangerous than the 'red' anarchist who would, if he could, overthrow all government. That can never be done, but the despotism of unbridled passion may very easily take the place of the orderly and measurably just reign of statutory and constitutional law."

- *Ibid.*

Police brutality, when unwarranted, is a violation of civil rights, and Adventists even in 1900 understood this. Today, however, a good many would ignore the brutality of law enforcement, when we should hold to them an even higher standard than regular citizenry. Many see rioters and looters as the greater threat when in fact the opposite is true. You can expect the lawless to commit lawless acts. But while rioters are a threat to order and civil peace, greater is the threat of lawmen using their authority to commit abuses, and the dangerous thing is that many will not see it coming.

Of course, it is expected that law enforcement will use some measure of force to curb lawlessness. Romans 13 bears this out. But even in this there are rules to be followed, and civil rights to be respected. Lawmen are not above the law. A suspected criminal still needs to go through the due process of law, a judge, jury, and then when appropriate, the executioner. When this constitutional process is not followed, one can expect there to be social upheavals in protest. Law enforcement officers should be held to higher standards, just like a Christian must be held to a higher spiritual and moral standard.

The vast majority of law enforcement officers are honorable. This is why when officers abuse their authority, it is even more egregious because it will reflect upon their profession and their comrades.

Just like the lure of money, the temptations that come with power multiply. Beware of the anarchist that comes under the guise of "law and order."

Chapter Five:

The Three Angels' Message, Racial Prejudice, and the Immigrant

Racial prejudice is a problem in the world. In the United States, our history has been marked with intense racial struggle, from slavery to Jim Crow, from Civil Rights to racial profiling that has raised its ugly head in more recent times. There are, however, circles within our Adventist midst that wish to dismiss these issues, using dismissive pejoratives such as "social justice," "political correctness," or saying these things have no bearing on our message as Seventh-day Adventists. Some even dare to suggest there is no spiritual benefit to upholding the rights of all.

But is this true? Or is the truth more complex than some make it out to be? Of course, in the hyperpolitical atmosphere of today's world, there is a tendency and temptation to create partisan divides that tend to foster unnecessary divisions that are not conducive to the spread of the Gospel. We are warned against making issues out of partisan political divisions that cause the message of the Third Angel to flounder.

Ellen White wrote,

> *"God's children are to separate themselves from politics, from any alliance with unbelievers. Do not take part in political strife. Separate from the world, and refrain from bringing into the church or school ideas that will lead to contention and disorder. Dissension is the moral poison*

> *taken into the system by human beings who are selfish.*"

> - *Counsels to the Church,* pg. 316.

Indeed, this is a problem in our churches today, with political questions all too often dominating our congregations' conversations. However, there are some conversations that need to be had, that are not a matter of politics, but of simple humanity and Biblical justice. Yes, some of these issues can eventually take on a political hue, but at bottom the nature of these issues is not political at all, but of justice and fairness, and of civil peace.

There are many who wish to sweep these issues "under the rug," ostensibly to keep the focus on the message of the Church, but such issues are to a degree that can no longer be ignored or dismissed.

One major issue I am talking about is racial prejudice. Automatically, many are going to recoil in horror that a Present Truth believer would cover this very incendiary subject, especially here in North America. The topic of race has been at the forefront of political news for as long as many can remember.

In the Spring of 2020, it came to the forefront again, with the murder of George Floyd, a black man killed in broad daylight during his arrest and in full view of many passing citizens. It has garnered national outrage, rightfully so, and has quickly become an issue of race and police brutality. The arresting officers were not all white, but the officer who had his knee on Floyd's neck, Derek Chauvin, was white. The publicly recorded and shared videos showed a subdued Floyd helpless and pleading with (now ex) Officer Chauvin who seemed unrelenting and without compassion kept his knee on his neck for almost a full eight minutes.

Minneapolis moved swiftly to terminate the officers involved, but the damage had already been done. Chauvin was later arrested for murder, but the incident sparked protests nationwide, creating chaos and mayhem. It brought back into the spotlight the conversation of race relations and the question of racial profiling. There are questions about whether Floyd would have been treated in that manner had he been amember of another race.

The same question was brought up in another case that dominated the headlines that year where Ahmaud Arbery, a young black man, was killed by white men in Georgia. The list of names of those whose lives ended before their time due to apparent profiling, meaning they would likely have lived had their race been different, is long. Eric Garner, Philando Castile, Jordan Edwards,Botham Jean, Atatiana Jefferson, and Breonna Taylor…and the list goes on.

Many are uncomfortable talking about racial profiling. Some deny it exists, some say it's a political ploy, and some say discussing it detracts from our message as Seventh-day Adventists.

But should we shy away from the topic, simply because it has been politicized by those with their own agendas? Can we not address the Biblical and Christian principles involved while at the same time avoiding the incendiary political rhetoric that poisons most discussions of these important topics? These topics are Biblical issues that bind upon us as Christians, known by many as the "Golden Rule."

> *"Therefore all things whatsoever ye would that men should do to you, do ye even so to them: for this is the law and the prophets."*

- Matthew 7:12 KJV

The topic of racial equality is not a question of politics, it is a question of simple Biblical fairness and justice. Do not believe the so-called "Biblical Christians" who try to argue otherwise. Most of these have been complacent in their privilege and have become uncomfortable with anything that unsettles the status quo for the racial hierarchy that has been ingrained in the soul of the nation and cherished in the institutions of slavery and segregation during a large portion of our history.

So no, this is not a question of politics. At least it

should not be. It is a simple issue of justice in light of aChristian's duty to treat his fellow man as he would like to be treated, no matter the skin-color, economic status or professed religion.

It is often pointed out that more whites are killed by police overall. While this is true, it is misleading, since there are, obviously, many more whites than blacks in America. This is evident, given that there is

> *"evidence of a significant bias in the killing of unarmed black Americans relative to unarmed white Americans, in that the probability of being black, unarmed, and shot by police is about 3.49 times the probability of being white, unarmed, and shot by police on average."*

- Cody T. Ross, "A Multi-Level Bayesian Analysis of Racial Bias in Police Shootings at the County-Level in the United States, 2011–2014," *PLOS ONE*, November 2015.

Also,

> "*African Americans are more than twice as likely as white drivers to be searched during vehicle stops even after controlling for non-race-based variables such as the reason the vehicle stop was initiated, but are found in possession of contraband 26% less often than white drivers, suggesting officers are impermissibly considering race as a factor when determining whether to search...*"

- *US Department of Justice - Civil Rights Division*, "Investigation of the Ferguson Police Department," 4 March 2015.

Even more telling is this study done in 2015 which said,

> "*...officers were more likely to stop black drivers for no*

discernible reason. And they were more likely to use force if the driver was black, even when they did not encounter physical resistance."

- Sharon LaFraniere and Andrew W. Lehren, "The Disproportiate Risks of Driving While Black," *New York Times*, 25 October 2015.

There is a prejudice in the mind of the nation that permeates even into the psyche of law enforcement, creating undue bias in tense situations. And this prejudice also extends past the law enforcement community to the nation at large because although we have advanced in leaps and bounds since slavery was abolished, we have failed to address the issue of racism at its core.

The Seventh-day Adventist Church needs to be relevant and involved in this discussion as we are the most racially diverse religious group in America, and have a significant presence around the world, representing many cultures and peoples. See:

- Michael Lipka, "The most and least racially diverse U.S. religious groups," *Pew Research*, 27 July 2015.

We cannot make gains in the cause of racial equality if we show even the slightest sympathy for those that perpetrate racial prejudice, or if we dismiss it as being "political." We were once at the forefront of the abolitionist movement to abolish slavery. We opened our homes to runaway slaves on the Underground Railroad. We disobeyed the Fugitive Slave Act and called for the racial equality of the black race. Would you call these efforts "political"? Or perhaps this article from the *Review and Herald* in 1865 written by James White was being "political" when it foretold:

> "Slavery will be dead only in name. It will still exist in fact. There will still be bondmen in this land, bound in fetters of

*disfranchisement, proscription
and prejudice, more galling and
oppressive than the iron
manacles that have heretofore
clanked upon their bleeding
limbs."*

- James White, *Review and Herald*, June 20,1865.

Just like our Pioneers were at the forefront of the 19th century abolitionism, Seventh-day Adventists today must be in the forefront of opposing the disfranchisement, proscription and prejudice of minorities today. It is not a political issue; it is a moral imperative.

Sure, the solution is best if aimed at the heart, as we will see in a later chapter. But the Church can do this by issuing a straight-to-the-heart rebuke of racial prejudice and disfranchisement and stop dismissing the issue and sweeping it under the rug as another "sin" that will be around until Jesus comes. If we are to call out sin by its right name, then it is part of our Biblical calling to condemn the modern-day iteration of slavery!

How can the Gospel message of the Three Angels' go to "every nation, and kindred, and tongue, and people" if we have at best tolerated, or at worst perpetuated the prejudice and disfranchisement of the same?

If we encourage silence or passiveness upon this matter, we will be judged guilty by these, and our attempts to evangelize them will only have an ill effect. How can we preach of a Heaven where prejudice does not exist and yet stand idly by as that same prejudice is displayed on this earth? God's People can no longer besilent. They can no longer stand by.

In an article entitled *The Three Angels of Rev. XIV, 6-12*, J. N. Andrews takes aim at the United States' institution of slavery as part of the injustices of the "two-horned beast":

> *"If all men are born free and equal, why then does this power hold three millions of human beings in the bondage of slavery? Why*

> is it that the Negro race is
> reduced to the rank of chattels
> personal, and bought and sold
> like brute beasts?"

-   John N. Andrews, *Review and Herald*,
    April 3, 1855.

Ellen White herself wrote in the *Review*:

> "The neglect of the colored race
> by the American nation is
> charged against them...Many
> among this race have noble traits
> of character and keen
> perception of mind. If they had
> an opportunity to develop, they
> would stand upon an equality
> with the whites."

-   Ellen G. White, *Review and Herald*,
    December 17, 1895.

James White, John Andrews, Joseph Bates and many of the Adventist Pioneers, including Ellen White, saw that resolving the issue of racial injustice was essential to the cause of the Third

Angels' Message. Ellen White even rebuked the inadequacy of the government in aiding the blacks after their emancipation:

> *"Much might have been accomplished by the people of America if adequate efforts in behalf of the freedmen had been put forth by the Government and by the Christian churches immediately after the emancipation of the slaves. Money should have been used freely to care for and educate them at the time they were so greatly in need of help. But the Government, after a little effort, left the Negro to struggle, unaided, with his burden of difficulties...But how few have had a part in this work which should have had the sympathy and help of all!"*

- Ellen G. White, *Testimonies*, Vol. 9, pg. 205.

If they didn't know Ellen White penned this statement, many would decry this as a "political," "socialist," "social justice warrior" mentality that has nothing to do with our message. But then, they don't know our message. The fact that literal slavery as an institution no longer exists does not diminish our obligation to confront racial prejudice wherever it is found. Those that suggest otherwise are not in line with our prophetic message and identity, no matter the lip-service they give to the truth. The callousness of their disregard for minorities in their plights socially and economically speak volumes.

Our message is intended for every individual on this earth. This is the commission given to us by Christ, to preach a message of liberty and freedom from sin. And we cannot do that while we tolerate the sin of racial prejudice in our midst or in the world at large. There is a lot of hurt stemming from a system of prejudice long tolerated in this country. And while we disagree and cannot condone the methods some use to express it, we can understand the resentment that has formed over many, many decades.

We must sympathize with the pain, but also encourage a response tempered by compassion and intellect. But we must never, ever dismiss this issue. Those that perpetrate prejudice must be confronted, as with a bully or abuser, in a firm and uncompromising stance stating that their behavior will no longer be tolerated. Not unlike Christ who confronted the spiritual abuse of the Pharisees of His day.

> *"Ye serpents, ye generation of vipers, how can ye escape the damnation of hell?"*

Christ demanded of them in Matthew 23:33.

God dealt with the institution of slavery decisively, and even punished the North for long tolerating and enduring its presence. May this not be our lot for this day, and may we confront with boldness the modern slavery of disfranchisement, proscription and prejudice.

Another aspect of racism is evident in nativism, a curious revulsion of immigrants. The term "nativist" refers to a political movement that arose in the 1840's, and it didn't refer to Native Americans, but to the descendants of the Thirteen Colonies, and theyopposed immigration and wanted to maintain the ethnical and racial homogeneity of America. Irish, German, and Chinese immigrants were all victims of prejudice due to this political scheme in the 1800's.

In the 21st Century, we have seen the revival of this movement, this time against immigrants from the Third World, especially those south of the border.

"Well, actually," you might object, "I'm not against immigrants, just illegal immigrants."

This is a curious inconsistent attitude, because there are tens of thousands of Canadians living illegally in the United States, yet the political rhetoric is directed at mostly Hispanics, and the nativists want a "wall" built on the southern border, not the northern one. This is racial prejudice.

And what about a Christian's attitude towards

what Emma Lazarus wrote were the "tired, poor, huddled masses yearning to breathe free"? What about the legacy of the forefathers of the American nation, seeking refuge from the religious and civil persecution they experienced in Europe?

It is a shame that nativist prejudice still exists and permeates American society today. A popular meme had been going around that stated, "Heaven has closed borders, Hell has open borders. Think about that!"

This is a gross misconstruction of reality and blurring of the distinct lines between the civil government of the United States, and the Kingdom of Heaven. Aside from its blasphemous connotations, it uses the element of fear and intimidation to scare people, especially those of a Christian persuasion, into taking a political position against immigration.

What does the Bible have to say on the matter?

> *"Cursed is the one who perverts*
> *justice for the resident foreigner,*

65

the orphan, and the widow.'
Then all the people will say,
'Amen!'"

- Deuteronomy 27:19 NET

"Thus says the Lord of hosts:
Render true judgments, show
kindness and mercy to one
another; do not oppress the
widow, the orphan, the alien, or
the poor; and do not devise evil in
yourhearts against one another."

- Zechariah 7:9-10 NRSV

Much of the nativist resentment today is born out of false narratives and propaganda. The Bible also has a lot to say about bearing false witness. But even if illegal immigrants do somehow "steal our jobs," "get free welfare," "don't pay taxes," or anything else the propaganda machine dishes, there is no Biblical mandate that we, as Christians, are to sympathize with the rounding up of illegal immigrants on trains and packing them in detention gulags for deportation.

America is a land of refuge, a land which God blessed. To horde the blessings for oneself and to keep the rest of humanity from experiencing them is a crime against humanity, and a sin against the God of Heaven.

Does Heaven have closed borders?

One thing our simplistic meme did not mention, the borders of Heaven are closed, but to *sin*, not to people. Only those that wish to carry their sins with them will be barred from the Kingdom. The Bible is clear, Heaven will be a place for all nations:

> *"After these things I looked, and behold, a great multitude which no one could number, of all nations, tribes, peoples, and tongues, standing before the throne and before the Lamb, clothed with white robes, with palm branches in their hands, and crying out with a loud voice, saying, 'Salvation belongs to our God who sits on the throne, and to the Lamb!'"*

\- Revelation 7:9-10 NKJV

Chapter Six:

Justice, the Working Class, and the Poor

We cannot continue our discussion about justice without mentioning those that are economically disadvantaged. Dealing with economics is within the purview of civil government, so there are elements within this discussion that may be considered by some as political, understandably so. However, we need to acknowledge that at bottom, the treatment of disadvantaged people is a matter of righteousness and morality, not merely civil.

Therefore, it is apropos to discuss the matter of the economically disadvantaged in very scriptural and spiritual terms. Adventists are very apprehensive aboutthe nature of a Sunday Law, a part and parcel of the denomination's Historicist eschatological understanding of Daniel and Revelation. In the book of Revelation, prophecy does hint at economic ruin for the Beast power in chapter 18:

> *10 Standing afar off for the fear of her torment, saying, Alas, alas that great city Babylon, that mighty city! for in one hour is thy judgment come.*
>
> *11 And the merchants of the earth shall weep and mourn over her; for no man buyeth their merchandise any more:*
>
> *12 The merchandise of gold, and silver, and precious stones, and of pearls, and fine linen, and purple, and silk, and scarlet, and*

all thyine wood, and all manner vessels of ivory, and all manner vessels of most precious wood, and of brass, and iron, and marble,

13 And cinnamon, and odours, and ointments, and frankincense, and wine, and oil, and fine flour, and wheat, and beasts, and sheep, and horses, and chariots, and slaves, and souls of men.

14 And the fruits that thy soul lusted after are departed from thee, and all things which were dainty and goodly are departed from thee, and thou shalt find them no more at all.

15 The merchants of these things, which were made rich by her, shall stand afar off for the fear of her torment, weeping and wailing,

16 And saying, Alas, alas that great city, that was clothed in fine linen, and purple, and scarlet, and decked with gold, and precious stones, and pearls! For in one hour so great riches is come to nought. And every shipmaster, and all the company in ships, and sailors, and as many as trade by sea, stood afar off,

17 And cried when they saw the smoke of her burning, saying, What city is like unto this great city!

18 And they cast dust on their heads, and cried, weeping and wailing, saying, Alas, alas that great city, wherein were made rich all that had ships in the sea by reason of her costliness! for

in onehour is she made desolate.

19 Rejoice over her, thou heaven, and ye holy apostles and prophets; for God hath avenged you on her.

This apocalyptic prophecy on the desolation of Babylon is poetic justice; she deals in "slaves, and souls of men" among the many other material riches with which she has fattened herself in profit.

The language used by the Bible is by no means redemptive in dealing with Babylon; she has filled her cup of iniquity, and her time of reckoning has come. It is of interest that the merchants dealing with her weep as she is overcome by plague and destruction.

The Colonial Era saw the spread of civilization and the Christian faith, but often through means of cultural subjugation and class oppression. Slavery became a significant part of the world economy, and the New World especially used that abusive and oppressive system to build its economy.

Thankfully, God retained a conscientious people, who through learned hardships and trial found exact justice and compassion to be an essential part of Christian duty. Whether it was to petition for liberty of conscience, or for the freedom of all and equality of men before God, the Remnant of God sought at every avenue to break chains and loose captive souls.

In the 21st Century we boast of having an advanced civilization with the best technologies known in history, yet oppression continues to exist, economically.

Capitalism, an economic system built upon the idea of a free market, has its virtues. Still, like every humanly- devised system, it also has its limitations and weaknesses, some even glaring, as we will see in later chapters. The drive to lower costs while driving up profits is a potential recipe for oppression. Adventists in the early 1900's saw dangers in socialism, yet also saw the need to temper those who swore by a free market system as the answer to all economic woes. Their dedication to balance is incredible:

> *"The capitalist who 'sweats' his employees at the expense of their health in order that he may selfishly add to his ever-increasing income, is as culpable as the Bolshevik who takes the capitalist's property away and turns him adrift without means and without physical ability to undertake hard labour in order to support himself and his dependents. Neither are right and neither can endure; for both these courses and both these purposes set man against man; and the inevitable sequence is turmoil and strife, bitterness and hatred, war and bloodshed."*

– C. M. Snow, *Signs of the Times Australia,* November 17, 1919.

An unbalanced view of economics will certainly lead to extremes. Sweeping such issues aside will not keep us from the moral reckoning that is to follow if we do not harken to inspired statements on the matter. The Bible and the Spirit of Prophecy are clear that greed, labor and wage theft are egregious sins.

Partisan pundits, in and outside the church, will squabble over the issue on one side or the other. But the plain truth is that people suffer for want of necessities, and civil policies relative to financial issues can make or break a person's ability to eat. Charity alone is not enough, and even Christ Himself admonished us to render unto Caesar that which is Caesar's, while submitting unto God that which is God's. Christ would not support the anarchist tendencies of many today who view taxation as inherently evil.

Today's Caesar, or the civil governments of the 21st century, may not always be perfect. But they serve a purpose under the heavens, and that is to maintain civilorder on earth. Inevitably financial dealings will fall under this purview, given that a people deprived of necessities and means by manipulation, deception, or coercion will likely become discontented and react against those with plenty.

While Sodom is today typically associated with sexual immorality and hedonism—and rightly so, according to the Bible (Jude 7)—another verse that outlines the specific sins of that city-state is found in Ezekiel 16:49,which states:

> *"Behold, this was the iniquity of thy sister Sodom, pride, fulness of bread, and abundance of idleness was in her and in her daughters, neither did she strengthen the hand of the poor and needy."*

You don't see this verse quoted much, if at all, by Christians who seem to favor capitalism unrestrained by civil government. It is a wonder why, because many of these same Christians tend to decry the debased morals and hedonism seen today, often comparing these with the immorality of ancient Sodom. This is irony at its finest.

But might there be a solution that does not involve hyper-partisan politics? It's simpler than it is made outto be. A combination of free market policies and social safety nets has worked well historically. For all the inspired statements warning against the rise of labor unions, such can be avoided if employers treated their workers fairly and justly.

Ellen White writes:

> "Like Abraham, he commanded his household after him to keep the way of the Lord to do justice and judgment. He showed courtesy to all his servants, and as he passed among his workmen in the field, he said unto the reapers, 'The Lord be with you. And they answered him, The Lord bless thee.' Here is a lesson for both masters and servants,

for employers and the employed. The servants are strengthened in their hearts to do righteously, to be faithful to masters who manifest respectful kindness and courtesy towards them. Christians should be the most courteous people in the world."

- Ellen G. White, *The Home Missionary,* December 1, 1894

Labor unions arose out of the perceived abuse of the working class by employers, who under free market principles have often taken advantage of their workers by seeking maximum profit through—among other things—lowering the quality of working conditionsand salaries.

Back in the Middle Ages, feudalism kept peasants subservient to lords and nobles. After notable upheavals in society, the mentality of the working class changed; the foundations of church-state union were shaken, feudalism was rendered obsolete, and the Enlightenment ushered in an era of civil liberty that the working class saw as an opportunity to improve their status and conditions.

But before we indict the working classes for demanding more of their employers, we need to understand the historical context of those upheavals that led to very undesirable events, such as the French Revolution.

In a sense, the French Revolution had roots in the Enlightenment similar to those of the American Revolution: oppressive monarchies that saw the lower classes as less than equals. In the case of the American Revolution the colonies were not given adequate representation so far as governance was concerned, while in the French Revolution abuses of united church and state led to a peasant uprising that sought LIBERTÉ, ÉGALITÉ, FRATERNITÉ, as first expressed by Maximilien Robespierre, the architect of the Reign of Terror.

Robespierre, while desiring good reforms that reflected the liberty-and-equality virtues of his

American counterparts, embarked on a murderous crusade, using imprisonment and the guillotine to eliminate his opposition. Possessed with a devilish bloodthirsty agenda, the French Revolutionaries went on a rampage that their American counterparts never even dreamed of, killing political opponents and clergy.

In contrast, the Americans fought a gentleman's war of independence, guaranteed religious freedom as a solution to the ills of church-state union, and prospered without much violence relating to transitions of power throughout its history so far, thanks to governmental checks and balances. America is far from perfect, but she has a self-correcting system built into her Constitution.

The underpinnings of the discontent that triggered the French Revolution can be found in American society even today. In an earlier chapter we discussed systemic racism. It is of note that no inspired writing suggests that that particular issue will be resolved to a level that will ever be satisfactory to all. Discontent will continue to abound because oppression continues to abound, and it has been evident in society ever since the Fall of Man.

If there is any doubt, the Scriptures propose no real civil solution. An earthly utopia is not possible, because the hearts of men persist in their preference for evil over good.

However, the laws of civil societies in Caesar's sphere are expected to uphold societal peace and justice, imperfect though they are. At the very least, Christians should think twice about politically opposing civil movements seeking to minimize oppression; that is not the work of the Bible believer, and we will damage our witness. We can expect that unbelievers will try to find a worldly solution to their grievances, and we cannot blame them for doing so. The work of the Bible believer, then, is to empathize with their suffering, acknowledge the oppression, and point people to the source of true liberty and freedom from bondage—the Gospel of Jesus Christ.

The Gospel changes lives and creates new hearts

through the Holy Spirit; a mind imbued with the Spiritwill seek to treat others as they would like to be treated(Matt. 7:12), will reform characters to recoil from the very thought of superiority over fellow humans, and will emulate the example of Christ who came to serve, not to be served.

Yet it must be remembered that if we trivialize the suffering of others, or even oppose movements designed to provide balance and fairness into society, we will shut the door to our witness to them.

It would behoove us to consider the example of Jesus when dealing with the oppressed of society. He rebuked the proud and haughty Pharisees and Sadducees, told an unwilling young rich man to sell all his belongings to give to the poor, and spent His time among the rejected of society. If only that could be said about today's Christians. Today there are political movements seeking to relieve humansuffering, yet many contemporary Christians side with those seeking to build earthly wealth at the expense of the working class.

It is shameful that these secular movements, which may at times possess traits and characteristics that Christians cannot agree with, are the ones seeking justice and equality for all. The cynical will argue that the strategy is a type of "virtue signaling," to acquire the sympathy of the masses in a conspiracy to control more people.

Even if this were so, Christians should be even more compassionate and concerned about equality and justice for all than far-left secular radicals and humanists. Instead, many Christians are putting themselves out as friends to oppressors and materialists, thereby diluting the effectiveness of the Gospel to penetrate into the souls of men and women hardened by toil and the weight of economic and cultural prejudice and oppression.

Before his death, the great Martin Luther King, Jr. worked on a campaign to alleviate the sufferings of the economically oppressed. Having already spearheaded the great American Civil Rights movement, with racial equality gaining mainstream status, King aimed at the growing problem of poverty in the American nation.

The Poor People's March was conducted in 1968, in a brief moment before King's tragic assassination on April 4, 1968. The Poor People's Campaign was aimed at alleviating the conditions of the less fortunate, a movement that sadly stalled after King's death.

Despite King's constant call for nonviolent demonstration, acts of street violence and rioting still occurred, with a particular outburst occurring on March 28, 1968, which played into the strategy of the FBI to discredit King:

> "The FBI seized upon the March 28 violence as a way to undercut King's reputation as a man of peace and nonviolence. There is good reason to conjecture that the FBI's inaction on March 28 in the face of threatened mayhem was a deliberate decision on the part of bureau agents."

- Gerald McKnight, *The Last Crusade: Martin Luther King, Jr., the FBI, and the Poor People's Campaign,* 1998, ppg. 60–61.

King was clear on his reasons for nonviolence, and stated so in a manuscript he wrote that was only published a day after his death, *The Showdown for Nonviolence*:

> *"We really feel that riots tend to intensify the fears of the white majority while relieving its guilt, and so open the door to greater repression."*

- Martin Luther King, Jr., *The Showdown for Nonviolence,* 1968.

However, in the same manuscript he also appealed to the United States government to solve the problem of systemic economic inequality in order to avoid the inflaming of tempers:

> *"I'm committed to nonviolence absolutely...I will continue to preach it and teach it...But I'm frank enough to admit that if our nonviolent campaign doesn't generate some progress, peopleare just going to engage in more violentactivity..."*

- *Ibid.*

Here King states he is absolutely committed to nonviolence but recognizes that if tempers flare because of a lack of progress in economic and racial justice, there would be little he or anyone could do to stem the whirlwind of violence wrought in response to systemic oppression.

Ellen G. White predicted the same when she wrote on August 13, 1899:

> *"In India, China, Russia, and the cities of America, thousands of men and women are dying of starvation. The monied men, because they have the power,*

control the market. They purchase at low rates all they can obtain, and then sell at greatly increased prices. This means starvation to the poorer classes, and will result in a civil war. There will be a time of trouble such as never was since therewas a nation."

- Ellen G. White, *Manuscript 114*, 1899.

Since Ellen White wrote these prophetic words we have seen this come to pass. India revolted against the British Empire because of oppression, China and Russia saw bloody Communist revolutions against the bourgeoisie, and America has likewise struggled with racial and economic inequality. But while Ellen White did not endorse the violent reactions of the poorer classes, she does identify where the original atrocity begins—at thehouse of greed.

No wonder Paul writes in 1 Timothy 6:

9 But they that will be rich fall

into temptation and a snare, and into many foolish and hurtful lusts, which drown men in destruction and perdition.

10 For the love of money is the root of all evil: which while some coveted after, they have erred from the faith, and pierced themselves through with many sorrows.

11 But thou, O man of God, flee these things; and follow after righteousness, godliness, faith, love, patience, meekness.

And James writes in James 5:

1 Go to now, ye rich men, weep and howl for your miseries that shall come upon you.

2 Your riches are corrupted, and your garments are motheaten.

3 Your gold and silver is cankered; and the rust of them shall be a witness against you, and shall eat your flesh asit were fire. Ye have heaped treasure together for the last days.

4 Behold, the hire of the labourers who have reaped down your fields, which is of you kept back by fraud, crieth: andthe cries of them which have reaped are entered into the ears of the Lord ofsabaoth.

5 Ye have lived in pleasure on the earth, and been wanton; ye have nourished your hearts, as in a day of slaughter.

6 Ye have condemned and killed the just; and he doth not resist you.

Ellen White writes,

"Great evils result from the continued accumulation of wealth by one class, and the poverty of another. The sense of this oppression would arouse the passions of the poorer class. There would be a feeling of despair and desperation which would tend to demoralize society and open the door to crimes of every description. The regulations that God established were to promote social equality."

- Ellen G. White, *From Eternity Past*, pg. 384.

Don't take singular counsel, deprived of context, as a political point to reject civil welfare altogether. We know that Inspiration does not forbid Caesar from interfering in providing welfare for its needy citizens, at least those who are truly in need. We know Sister White encouraged government (and church) economic intervention in certain instances:

"Much might have been accomplished by the people of America if adequate efforts in behalf of the freedmen had been put forth by the Government and by the Christian churches immediately after the emancipation of the slaves. Money should have been used freely to care for and educate them at the time they were so greatly in need of help."

- Ellen G. White, *Testimonies*, Vol. 9, pg. 205.

Sister White refers to two types of "poor," those who are truly in need of material help, due to "sickness and misfortune," and the "unworthy poor" who seek to be dependent (see *Welfare Ministry*). Welfare needs to be dispensed only with qualifications, and above that, education must be given to the poor classes on how they can create industry and make a living for themselves. Both the church and state will greatlybenefit society with this process.

I have personally benefited from welfare in the past, from both church and government, so I know how much help it can be for those in a tough spot. I also know for a fact that it isn't usually being dispensed with no qualifications. I had to prove my need. Once I was able to provide an adequate income for myself and my family, I no longer qualified, and was dropped out from the program. Therefore, let's not believe every political propaganda piece out there.

One thing is clear, we should not look down on those less financially fortunate. And campaigning for or against either wholesale socialism or unfettered capitalism is not a divine imperative. We will see the relations of these systems with the Beast in the next chapter.

Chapter Seven:
The Nature of the
Beast

As pointed out previously, Adventist pioneers consistently saw elements of the dragon-speak of the United States of America in their day. Still, America was the most blessed of modern nations because of her status as a place of civil and temporal refuge where there was freedom to dwell within the warm protection of our spiritual refuge, Jesus Christ. Says the prophet,

"The United States has been a refuge for the oppressed. It has been spoken of as the bulwark of religious liberty. God has done more for this country than for any other country upon which the sun shines. It has been marvelously preserved from war and bloodshed."

– Ellen G. White, *Review and Herald*, December 17, 1895

This, however, was only referring to the lamb-like attributes of the second beast of Revelation 13. The dragon-like attributes have also been a part of its identity since its inception. In the same article quoted above, Ellen White excoriates America for tolerating the sins of racism and slavery, often equating the enslaved African-Americans to the enslaved Israelites of old. She praises the sacrifice of the Northern soldiers,

"The graves of American sons

who had enlisted to deliver the oppressed race are thick in its soil. Many fell in death, giving their lives to proclaim liberty to the captives, and the opening of the prison to them that were bound."

- Ellen G. White, *Review and Herald*, December 17, 1885.

There will always be a Lamb vs. Dragon dichotomy in the United States until Jesus comes—those that seek freedom of conscience and equal and exact justice for all, versus those who use oppression to fulfill their lust for lucre, superiority, and power.

Many Adventists search in vain through the myriad of conspiracy theories rampant in contemporary political circles, trying to find the Beast in a secret cabal or forces of evil in the shadows. In reality, the Beast is in plain sight for all to see.

The Antichrist has been identified, even in the

early days of the Protestant Reformation. The papal system has merged paganism and Christianity since its beginnings, and also blended church and state starting with Emperor Justinian I's *Codex Justinianus* which was codified in 529 A.D., then brought into effect in 534, although it could not be practiced until four years later in 538, when Justinian's General Belisarius defeated a Gothic army which was besieging Rome.

When the Goths fled, the Roman code could be fully enforced, including,

> *"...that all affairs touching the Church shall be referred to the Pope, 'Head of all bishops, and the true and effective corrector of heretics."'*

> - George Croly, *The Apocalypse of St. John*, second edition. London: 1828, pg. 170.

Since then, the Roman papacy gained almost unopposed hegemony over Christian affairs, and, thanks to the force of civil law, effectively laid the foundation of the church-state union we see featured in medieval and early modern Europe.

The extreme injustice and persecution that befell pre- Reformation Christian groups such as the Waldenses and the Cathars was a result of this unholy meld, and the papacy, using the sword of the state, subjected perceived heretics to severe oppression and legalized murder.

Thus, along with the early Protestant Reformers and eschatological historicists, Adventists have consistentlypointed at papal Rome as the Biblical Antichrist, with ample justification from history and Holy Writ.

The Roman Catholic Church continues to be a source of religio-political punditry, making nations drink of the wine of her fornication, mixing the profane with the holy (Rev. 14:8; 18:2). She has consistently dabbledin immorality and licentiousness, from the slave trade to child molestation and abuse scandals...on top of her extra-scriptural ecclesiastical meddling with the Law ofGod, especially regarding the transferring of the sacredness of the Saturday Sabbath to Sunday. She also vacillates between social compassion and oppression.

It is a strange historic curiosity that those religiously oppressed and those oppressed for their ethnic and economic status have never quite developed anideological and fraternal bond. While there have been movements in certain eras of history, such as with the abolitionist movement in the 19th century that came close to establishing this bond for good, it never really took off.

This is because while freedom of religion and the equality of all beliefs before the eyes of civil law has become established Constitutional fact, racial and economic equality has not. What we have today is a disparity; Evangelical Christianity has become complacent with its power, and as it continues to develop social and cultural status it will increasingly ignore the plight of the poor and minorities.

There are many in the Remnant Church that eye "social justice" with suspicion, with the idea that it is a "Jesuit" or "Marxist" plot. This represents criticism leveled without an adequate knowledge of the historical context.

The current contemporary conception of "social justice" is a melding of ideas, although the term was first used in modern academic thought by the Jesuit scholar Luigi Taparelli, who utilized Thomist thought in creating his conception of social justice.

- See Thomas Behr, *Social Justice and Subsidiarity: Luigi Taparelli and the Origins of Modern Catholic Social Thought.*

There is a tendency for certain uninformed Adventists to see all social justice concepts as inherently "Marxist" or "Jesuit," thanks to conservative media and cynical conspiracy theories.

But when we dig deeper, we will find that Taparelli was critical not only of unfettered capitalism, but also of socialism, and wrote against the dangers of *both*. The Jesuits have always had a mixed bag of thinkers both Right and Left, as one tends to find in every other institution.

Today's idea of social justice, such as the radical idea of racial equality that men like Martin Luther King, Jr. advocated for, is different from Taparelli's view. In fact, social conservatives who opposed MLK's equality vision in his day applied Taparelli's Jesuit principles by attacking those that separated morality from civil law.

Taparelli did indeed help modern Catholic moral views evolve from its traditionally conservative stances, but he also criticized liberal ideology and secular socialism. Therefore, the Jesuit "social justice" concept is not synonymous or necessarily compatible with its modern secular counterpart.

In contrast to Taparelli's view, Alonzo T. Jones represented the classical Adventist view, by teaching that morality and civility were separate spheres, morality being what we owed only to God and civility being what we owed to fellow humans in the eyes of the law. To Jones, the best way to get the societal reforms that allowed people to treat each other civilly was to give complete religious liberty and freedom of conscience in the realm of morality, and only then setting civil boundaries that would help keep citizens from tangibly harming one another.

This explains the consistency in the actions of our Adventist pioneers, who while teaching believers to stay aloof from political matters as consistent with the principle of separating church and state, nevertheless remained active in opposing by word, pen, and action the oppressive nature of slavery and the proliferation of alcohol and intemperance.

While Taparelli and the Jesuits proposed welding morality and civility together as an obligation to "natural law," Adventists sought to respect both morality and civility in their respective spheres. The early Adventists had a better record in consistency with their line of thought and practice.

For example, the early Adventists were active in the abolitionist movement and smuggled slaves from their masters on the Underground Railroad, while the Jesuits owned a great number of slaves in the Americas. So much for *Jesuit* "social justice"!

> *"Clearly there was a wide and stark gap between official church doctrine and the commercial practice of individual Roman Catholics through the life of the slave trade. According to the historian David Eltis, 'The Roman Catholic Church was the largest single owner of slaves in the Americas.' And the Jesuits' sale of the 272 enslaved people at Georgetown was not an exception but rather the rule. As Eltis notes, 'The Jesuits, perhaps the largest corporate slave owners in the Americas (after the Catholic Church itself), relied almost exclusively on slave labor to work farms, cane lands, mines, vineyards, and textile*

mills, as well as ranches for cattle, sheep, and mules... The church's role in the slave trade was hypocritical, riddled with inconsistencies, and deeply, darkly shameful.'"

- Henry Louis Gates, Jr., *The Black Church.*

Even after Taparelli conceived of his notion of "social justice," the Catholic Church continued its practice of slave ownership, proving that Catholics were only interested in areas of "social justice" that benefited them.

Antebellum Southern Protestant slave-owners did themselves no favors by mirroring papal oppression in religious and social matters, justifying their slave ownership and racial superiority by twisting Scripture. Only a minority of American Christians became truly active in the abolition work, at least until the South seceded and aroused the anger of the North.

So, while the modern term "social justice" did have Jesuit roots, it is significantly different from its secular counterpart.

Capitalism is seen by many as a byproduct of the Protestant Reformation and the work ethic it inspired, although the historical truth is that capitalism had Catholic roots. Capitalism can be traced back to the monastic orders such as the Cistercian order. Prior to that, feudalism was the socio-economic system of the day, and was normal to most people living in medieval Europe.

The erroneous idea that capitalism was a product of Protestantism can be attributed to Max Weber's book, *The Protestant Ethic and the Spirit of Capitalism*. Many Western Protestants, including some Seventh- day Adventists, view capitalism as the bedrock of Protestant and American society.

While private industry is never condemned in the Bible or the Spirit of Prophecy, it would be a gross exaggeration, and indeed an extra-biblical suggestion, to imply that capitalism is a divine imperative.

Weber wrote his thesis in 1905; since then, many researchers have dug deeper and found that capitalism has darker roots, beginning with medieval Catholicism. Weber believed that Protestants pioneered the capitalist work ethic, but others disagree:

> *"I intend to argue, on the contrary, that the Middle Ages experience, the key institutional revolution, that the basis of capitalism was laid then rather than later, and that at its heart was the organization of the Catholic Church itself."*

> \- Randall Collins, *Weberian Sociological Theory*, pg. 45.

Collins' objection to Weber's thesis is not without a good basis. Hundreds of years before Luther and Calvin, the Cistercian Order began the money-making corporate work ethic. The Cistercians were a splinter group of the

Benedictine Order.

They took a strict vow of poverty, but soon found themselves at odds with that vow. They had a policy of leaving no monk idle, and productivity soared. Products were produced and even after the poor and local population were well provided for there was a giant surplus. Nothing was allowed to go to waste, so the Cistercians engaged in trade, establishing a huge amount of monetary wealth.

Since the Cistercians took a strict vow of poverty and couldn't hang onto the money, they used it to buy swaths of land, which they used to farm and increase profits even further. In irony the Cistercians became a living contradiction, as many of them became very powerful through the wealth they initially sought to dispose of due to their strict vows, and a few Cistercian abbots became influential legates for the Pope. One, the Abbot Arnaud Amalric, even led the Albigensian Crusade, ordering the attack on the town of Béziers in which 20,000 men, women, and children were massacred, many of whom were not just heretics, but Catholics, killed in cold blood even after armed resistance ceased.

Historian James McDonald explains:

> *"At the beginning of the thirteenth century, the [Cistercian] order had existed for just over a century. In that century it had grown from a tiny pocket of impoverished break-away Benedictine monks who renounced the world, into a massive, successful, rich, powerful, worldly multinational corporation that excelled in two separate fields - agriculture and religious warfare."*

- James McDonald, *Kill Them All: Did a Medieval Abbot give this Command to his Crusader Troops?*, pg. 29.

This was the origin of what President Dwight Eisenhower once warned was the "military industrial complex," a culture of private corporations looking to profit from war and human suffering.

Thanks to the power that wealth generates, we would see more and more evil done in the name of money—and falsely in the name of Christ. Spain and Portugal, wealthy Catholic nations, began enslaving Africans for use in private enterprises in the Americas. This was later spread to the colonial empires of the Dutch, French, and the English.

> *"True enough, the Transatlantic slave trade was not the only slavery that existed in the history of man's inhumanity to man...But the Transatlantic slave trade is different from all these...It was the only slave trade in human history that made the Black man its only victim and reduced him to a chattel. It was the only slave trade that carried its victims in ships of different sizes and*

shapes bearing the names of Virgin Mary, Jesus Christ, St. Thomas, St. George and other Saints ofthe Holy Roman Catholic Church."

- Pius Onyemechi Adiele, *The Popes, the Catholic Church and the Transatlantic Enslavement of Black Africans 1418-1839,* pg. 1,2.

Can anyone fault the Revelator for thus warning about Babylon?

"And the merchants of the earth shall weep and mourn over her; for no man buyeth their merchandise any more: The merchandise of gold, and silver...and slaves, and souls of men"

With money comes power. No wonder the Beast fills the cup of God's indignation to the brim, where itis about to overflow.

While many Adventists focus on an upcoming

112

Sunday Law, which no doubt *is* the great test of loyalty in the end time, what will lead so many to acquiesce to such a law is tolerance of an injustice towards our fellow humans. This is an abomination towards the God of Heaven.

> "The customs of the world are no criterion for the Christian. He is not to imitate their sharp practice, over- reaching, and extortion, even in small matters. Every unjust act toward a fellow-mortal, though he be the veriest sinner, is a violation of the golden rule. Every wrong done to the children of God, is done to Christ himself in the person of his saints. Every attempt to advantage one's self by the ignorance, weakness, or misfortune of another, is registered as fraud in the Ledger of Heaven."

- Ellen G. White, *Signs of the Times*,

December 20, 1883.

Do we not weep for our apathy towards our fellow mortals? If not, we are erecting our own image to the Beast, following in the footsteps of the Arch- Oppressor. We fear to speak out against injustice because we fear becoming "political." The abolitionist Adventists of the 19th century had no such qualms.

Since when did how we treat our fellow beings in fairness and justice become "political"? True Protestants do not merely protest the wrongs done against them and the Most High; they protest the wrongs done to those even not of their own tribe, caste,race, or belief.

The Beast is no stranger to oppressing people. Let us not give it any help by remaining apathetic or even antagonistic against claims of oppression. Our job is to stand up for the oppressed and to despise injustice in all its forms.

Chapter Eight:
Revival, Reformation, and the Closing of the Great Controversy

As we have seen in the preceding chapters, the three angels' messages (Rev. 14:6-12) is a warning not simply against erroneous doctrines and dogma, but against oppression of any kind, and it involves the revealing of God's character of love and justice to the whole universe.

The investigative judgment examines the lives of those who wish to be members of God's eternal kingdom. It is not only the outward acts but the innermost contents of the heart that are placed under intense scrutiny.

> *"Therefore, judge nothing before the time, until the Lord come, who both will bring to light the hidden things of darkness, and will make manifest the counsels of the hearts: and then shall every man have praise of God."*

- 1 Corinthians 4:5 KJV

Babylon the Great, as the papal system is called, has sins of a darker hue than the purple and scarlet she is decked with. With a record of atrocity and complicity in crimes against humanity and the God of heaven for over a millennium, she will finally meet her end at the coming of Christ.

But bear in mind that our eschatology by principle considers the difference between a system and its people. Throughout the ages there have been conscientious Roman Catholics, clergy and laity alike, that have stood up to oppression, even from their own leadership.

When the dreadful Crusader army was at the gates of Béziers in 1209, the townspeople were given the chance to surrender their "heretics," since there were many devout Catholics in the city. The Waldenses and the Cathars even volunteered to surrender to save the city from harm, but the Catholics of Béziers refused.

When the subsequent massacre took place, a great many Catholics were killed protecting the heretics; even Catholic priests giving Mass in an attempt shield the populace in churches, both Catholic and heretic, were cut down in a torrent of blood by Crusaders at the urging of the papal legate. The bloodlust of the Harlot would not be satisfied, and the Albigensian Crusade continued, as well as did the Inquisition and the Counter-Reformation centuries later.

We need to be able to differentiate conscientious Catholic believers and practitioners from the system of confusion that teaches the commandments and traditions of men. Our job is to call them out of Babylon, which is in a state of spiritual fallenness.

Babylon's wickedness is systemic, and deep within the Lamb-like Beast is also a systemic problem that has always been at odds with justice.

The Roman papacy has had its goblet dipped in the blood of the saints, and while she pays lip service to "social justice," she has refused to remove her hand from the jar of meddling in state affairs, using the fallible arm of flesh to enforce that which God alone has prerogatives to enforce.

Sadly, much of the Protestant world has followed suit. While Catholicism began the slave trade, many American Protestants were at the forefront of defending this despicable institution just prior to the Civil War. Protestants have been erecting an image to the Beast by supporting and continuing the elements of oppression, religious and civil, that have been initiated by the papal system. Catholics and many Protestants in America practiced racism during the era of slavery, reconstruction, and during the Jim Crow era. What a blight this has been on the name of Christianity!

All of this is part of the system put in place by the Mother of Harlots (Rev. 17:5), and practiced by her daughters. Sure, today's Catholicism is more tolerant, but even after Pius XI's explicit rejection of racism, Catholicism continues to fall behind in mending race relations in America, a fact evident from the statement of theologian James Cone who wrote,

> *"What is it about the Catholic definition of justice that makes many persons of that faith progressive in their attitude toward the poor in Central America but reactionary in their views toward the poor in black America? ...It is the failure of the Catholic Church to deal effectively with the problem*

of racism that causes me to question the quality of its commitment to justice in other areas."

- As quoted by Bryan M. Massingale, "James Cone and Recent Catholic Episcopal Teaching on Racism." *Theological Studies*, 61 (4): 700–730.

Cone realized the inconsistency of Rome in its commitment to resolving poverty and racism. Since Latin America has a higher percentage of Catholic believers, the poor from the rest of the world see a bias in how they are treated.

This is not to say the poor in the Latin countries should be ignored, it is to say that Rome has an agenda behind its ostensible benevolence and commitment to "social justice."

Yet we must ask, is the Remnant Church any better at tackling the problem of racism and ethnic prejudice that exists in her ranks and in the nation and the world at large? How many preachers of "Present Truth" thumb their nose at this movement to confront injustice today?

When Protestant Churches wrest control of civil government from secular forces in America, the forming of the image to the Beast will be completed:

> *"In order for the United States to form an image of the beast, the religious power must so control the civil government that the authority of the state will also be employed by the church to accomplish her own ends."*

> - Ellen G. White, *The Great Controversy*, pg. 443.

The nature of the Beast is one of oppression, religious and civil. Just as a literal beast is merciless in wounding and then devouring its prey, the Beast power will also be merciless in subjugating and destroying her victims.

This is in contrast to the loving, merciful character of Christ and His dedication to divine justice. The symbolic comparison is striking: Jesus, the meek Lamb of God, finally ending the murderous reign of the Beast and the Dragon.

We can safely assume that the issues of racial prejudice and oppression of the poorer classes are issues those of us concerned with the three angels' messages must be outspoken about.

Some are weary and afraid to speak out against oppression. They feel it is too unrelated to the Gospel. This is never so. If it were so, Inspiration would not be so rife with divine admonition to hate injustice and to treat one another with the same respect as we seek to be given.

> *"Injustice is in the highest degree displeasing to God."*

-   Ellen G. White, *Review and Herald*, June 24, 1902.

It is not a fact that can be overstated, and one that challenges us deep within our souls and forms ourcharacter. In order for there to be true revival and reformation, our hearts must be willing to have the compassion of our Savior, His character of mercy, and also of *justice*.

Jesus would tolerate no injustice to be done to anyone. When referring to the wicked who would abuse young children, Jesus, in no uncertain terms said,

> *"But whoso shall offend one of these little ones which believe in me, it were better for him that a millstone were hanged about his neck, and that he were drowned in the depth of the sea."*

> - Matthew 18:6 KJV

Seemingly shocking words from a Man that people see as meek and lowly. But true meekness is not the same as weakness, and Christ would never sit by and tolerate evil and injustice.

Many believe that Jesus took a whip of cords and chased the money changers out of the Temple court because they were desecrating the house of God. This is true, of course. But it is only part of the story. Christ's anger was aroused by the blatant injustice He saw dealt to the poor.

> "The money changers were displeased with His action. 'What business,' they questioned, 'had He to interrupt their work?' The stalls were their own; they had paid a sufficient sum for them to the temple authorities, that they might sell the sacrificial offerings to the people. Their hearts were full of avarice and selfishness. They had oppressed the poor, and the widow and fatherless, refusing to give them an offering at the small sum they could pay. When the poor had presented their distress to them, they had turned away as unfeelingly as though the poor had no souls to save. They had

> *pointed the finger of scorn at them, charging them with sin, and declaring that their suffering and poverty was curse from God on account of transgression. Men who could deal thus with the afflicted were not above planning the murder of the Son of God. And this they had done. On the way to the temple they had said they would kill the Saviour, and be rid of the troubler."*

- Ellen G. White, *Experiences in Australia*, pg. 190.

What many "Present Truth" preachers have failed to preach is that Christ's only burst of violence recorded in the Scriptures was in defense of His house of worship *and* justice for the poor and oppressed.

Greed and injustice were in the hearts of those who would later crucify Christ. The cold heart of oppression would be seen through history. When the papal system began the practice of paid indulgences, it was greed, not penitence, that drove this false commandment of men. It was a reaction to this greed and injustice that drove Martin Luther to pen his *95 Theses*, attacking the oppressive nature of indulgences, and challenging the authority of the Pope and the Church to pardon sins, which was the prerogative of God alone.

It was injustice and oppression, not merely false doctrine, that aroused the ire that gave rise to the Protestant Reformation, as it did with Christ in His interactions with the Pharisees.

False doctrines arise out of the selfishness within the human heart. They are a product of men enthroning themselves in the place of God. This idolatry mirrors the very character of Lucifer when he fell. Without God's presence in their lives, men and women will only seek to oppress and to deal unjustly.

The Great Controversy will close when Satan admits to the justice of his sentence. The God of mercy and justice will prevail. All those who have submitted to Satan and have mirrored his oppression will also receive their just reward.

> *"Satan sees that his voluntary rebellion has unfitted him for heaven. He has trained his powers to war against God; the purity, peace, and harmony of heaven would be to him supreme torture. His accusations against the mercy and justice of God are now silenced. The reproach which he has endeavored to cast upon Jehovah rests wholly upon himself. And now Satan bows down and confesses the justice of his sentence."*

\-   Ellen G. White, *The Great Controversy*, pg. 670.

The end of the Great Controversy will see the end of injustice and oppression, for none in the kingdom of God will seek to control or take advantage of their fellow beings. No one in the heavenly kingdom would seek to defraud, manipulate, or assume supremacy over their fellow heavenly citizens.

We talk of a revival of true godliness as our greatest need, and our first work. What in fact is true godliness? To have the character of God, His love and passion for justice. How about revival? True revival begins in the heart, and all hints of selfishness must be put away. Present Truth believers must share our God-given message for the final days with power, and to do so we must shed the cynicism and suspicion we have of movements and people seeking to create a better life for the oppressed.

Acknowledging and affirming the pain of those who feel marginalized by society and oppressed by those deemed "higher" on the societal ladder, will help our message resonate with those sidelined by circumstance.

After all, we can relate; injustice began at the heart of the Dragon, who empowers the Beast, and has persecuted and will persecute the saints in a campaign of oppression before the great and terrible Day of the Lord.

Chapter Nine:
The Solution

Christ and His righteousness is what we must seek. Yet too many hold to a theoretical embrace of this "righteousness" without feeling the obligation to have the mind and character of the Redeemer. Many attend lecture after lecture, listen to sermon after sermon, yet when the cries of the oppressed are raised, they ignore the plight of the needy, or denounce it as if it were the laugh of the devil.

When Christ was approached by the needy, high or low, we never saw an instance where He dismissed them with prejudice. The Gospel of Christ includes a warning against those who would abuse and oppress. The second angel's message is a warning of impending destruction upon Babylon, and as we shall discuss in the remaining chapters, Babylon is the source of all earthly oppression.

The Beast mirrors the character of the Dragon, who gives it its power and dominion. The Beast has subjugated the saints for too long. God is love, and because God is love, justice exists. You cannot have justice without love, because if you love someone you will seek justice for them when they are wronged.

In our individualistic culture in America, we have shunned community concern-driven policies and instead embraced the freedom to do as one wishes. This comes with advantages—and risks. With freedom comes power, and with power comes responsibility.

The solution to worldly ills is not a set of overarching legal policies or civil platitudes with a view to establishing an earthly utopia. The answer for the world's ills is Christ. A heart filled with Jesus by the Holy Spirit will not seek after one's own benefit, but for the benefit of all, in temporal and eternal matters.

As the song written by the late Gospel song writer Andraé Crouch goes, "Jesus is the Answer for the world today, above Him there's no other, Jesus is the Way." Indeed, Jesus is the Way, the Truth, and the Life.

Christ is the solution for the world, but how are we reflecting His character? By ignoring the plights of the less fortunate? God forbid.

Many of the brethren have brought up concerns with becoming involved in social issues due to the follow quotation, found in *The Desire of Ages*, page 509:

> *"The government under which Jesus lived was corrupt and oppressive; on every hand were crying abuses, —extortion, intolerance, and grinding*

cruelty. Yet the Saviour attempted no civil reforms. He attacked no national abuses, nor condemned the national enemies. He did not interfere with the authority or administration of those in power. He who was our example kept aloof from earthly governments. Not because He was indifferent to the woes of men, but because the remedy did not lie in merely human and external measures. To be efficient, the cure must reach men individually, and must regenerate the heart."

This is a beautiful passage, and it expresses without a doubt where the solution to the "woes of men" lies—the regeneration of the heart.

It is implied by many who criticize advocates of societal justice that because Christ attempted "no civil reforms" and that He "did not interfere with the authority or administration of those in power," that we are supposedly not to march in support of racial equality or economic justice, nor to preach, write, or even study it.

However, the same crowd likely applauds the triumph of republicanism over communism in the West, the victory of democracy over fascism in World War II, American independence from England, the abolition of slavery, the freedom of religion in the United States, and the right to free speech, all which were won on the temporal fields of military and political conflict.

Or, if those issues do not strike a chord in the minds of First World Adventists, how about Martin Luther's bold stand against the religio-political might and oppression of papal Rome, and the civil protests of the Lutheran princes at the Diet of Speyer in 1529, also known as the "Protestation of Speyer" from which the Reformers and their followers were thenceforth named "Protestants"?

On top of that, we have the example of the Seventh-day Adventist pioneers themselves, including the only one divinely inspired who wrote the passage in question: Ellen G. White, who was fully immersed in the abolitionist and prohibitionist causes.

We know for a fact that the abolitionist cause sought the social equality of African-Americans, not just their liberty, as seen in the preceding chapters.

Ellen G. White wrote:

> "I was taken off in vision and shown the sin of slavery, which has so long been a curse to this nation. The fugitive slave law was calculated to crush out of man every noble, generous feeling of sympathy that should arise in his heart for the oppressed and suffering slave. It was in direct opposition to the teaching of Christ. God's scourge is now upon the North, because they have so long submitted to the

advances of the slave power. The sin of Northern proslavery men is great. They have strengthened the South in their sin by sanctioning the extension of slavery; they have acted a prominent part in bringing the nation into its present distressed condition."

- Ellen G. White, *Testimonies for the Church*, Vol. 1, pg. 264.

In a call to actively interfere with the operation of the pro-slavery government, she wrote:

"The law of our land requiring us to deliver a slave to his master, we are not to obey; and we must abide the consequences of violating this law. The slave is not the property of any man. God is his rightful master, and man has no right to take God's workmanship into his hands, *and claim him as his own."*

- *Ibid.*, pg. 201.

In similar principle, we should resist and disobey a civil law to observe Sunday as a holy day.

Sister White, an abolitionist, consistently supported the call to end slavery, even at the cost of war. She never chided the North, except to denounce their delay in dealing with the issue decisively, to rebuke some Northern leaders who dabbled in spiritualism, as well as those who were looking to only preserve the Union while secretly sympathizing with the South on the slavery question.

This shows without a doubt that we, as the Remnant people of God, can and *should* be active in protesting injustice.

Yet when persons of conscience today decry the systemic racial and economic injustices that continue to exist to this day, they are derided and scorned, and then are thereafter accused of contradicting the Spirit of Prophecy, despite the insurmountable evidence that Sister White and the early Adventists used pen and voice to protest temporal injustices.

Beware those who call evil "good," and the good "evil."

If there was some *inspired* reason to abandon the endeavor to call out injustice, then why has it not been produced? There is no inspired evidence that commands us to turn a blind eye to human suffering.

We also have documented historical proof that the prohibitionist Adventists saw the prohibition of alcohol as not a mere spiritually moral issue, but also one of societal justice:

> *"But here is the great fact in the history of the past. Who has not seen the impatience of the drunkard? Some are very impatient as the brain is fired, and the spirit maddened with drink. See the wife and the children fleeing as they see the husband*

and father returning from his debauch."

- James White, *The Advent Review and Sabbath Herald*, April 9, 1867.

"When the appetite for spirituous liquor is indulged, the man voluntarily places to his lips the draft which debases below the level of the brute him who was made in the image of God. Reason is paralyzed, the intellect is benumbed, the animal passions are excited, and then follow crimes of the most debasing character."

– Ellen G. White, *Counsels for the Church*, pg.103.

Protection of the community, especially the weak and vulnerable, from the civil criminality and the emotional and physical abusiveness resulting from widespread alcohol usage, drove the social reform-minded Seventh-day

Adventists to vote for prohibitionist candidates—
a clear act of civil duty, and one that even Ellen G.
White saw no issues to take part in.

So, where does this leave us? If we abided only
by the quoted portion from *The Desire of Ages*,
we would think there was some conundrum, and
that Ellen White herself contradicted her own
writings in practice by calling for civil
disobedience against unjust and erroneous laws.

Only when one analyzes the *full context* of the
passage from *The Desire of Ages* will it be plain
what Inspiration is telling us as to why Jesus
refused to interfere with secular government.

Let us quote the paragraph preceding the passage:

> *"But today in the religious world*
> *there are multitudes who, as they*
> *believe, are working for the*
> *establishment of the kingdom of*
> *Christ as an earthly and*
> *temporal dominion. They desire*
> *to make our Lord the ruler of*
> *the kingdoms of this world, the*

ruler in its courts and camps, its legislative halls, its palaces and market places. They expect Him to rule through legal enactments, enforced by human authority. Since Christ is not now here in person, they themselves will undertake to act in His stead, to execute the laws of His kingdom. The establishment of such a kingdom is what the Jews desired in the days of Christ. They would have received Jesus, had He been willing to establish a temporal dominion, to enforce what they regarded as the laws of God, and to make them the expositors of His will and the agents of His authority. But He said, 'My kingdom is not of this world.' John 18:36. He would not accept the earthly throne."

We now see that she is talking about how that many, today, are seeking to join church and state *in an effort to establish a legal Christian morality in civil government.* Sister White states that these people will attempt to "to execute the laws of His kingdom" enforced by "human authority," which is in verity the nature of both Catholic and Protestant Babylon.

Then that is when she wrote, "The government under which Jesus lived was corrupt and oppressive..." Then immediately after that passage, we read:

> *"Not by the decisions of courts or councils or legislative assemblies, not by the patronage of worldly great men, is the kingdom of Christ established, but by the implanting of Christ's nature in humanity through the work of the Holy Spirit. 'As many as received Him, to them gave He power to become the sons of God, even to*

them that believe on His name:
which were born, not of blood,
nor of the will of the flesh, nor
of the will of man, but of God.'
John 1:12, 13. Here is the only
power that can work the
uplifting of mankind. And the
human agency for the
accomplishment of this work is
the teaching and practicing of the
word of God."

What we now see here is that the ultimate solution is Christ working in His people, and we are shown how the Gospel changes lives, the result of which is a people dedicated to fair and just treatment of their fellow humans. The whole context is a warning about joining Church and State. Yet it also becomes clear that Ellen White was not forbidding the conscientious person from speaking out against societal injustice. In actuality the passage from *The Desire of Ages* implores us to imitate Christ and abandon the call to join church and state, and the temptation to use "human authority" to enforce the laws of the kingdom of Christ. It does not prohibit us from speaking out against societal injustice.

Many conscientious Adventists cry out against the practice of abortion, but how many of the same cry out against systemic racism and economic oppression? To protest one injustice and ignore the others is a clear act of political partisanship.

To wit, it is expected of the Christian to teach and practice the Word of God, including the many calls to practice justice (Proverbs 21:3), to succor the widows and fatherless (James 1:27), and to call for the fair wages of laborers (James 5:4). To do this is in full consistency and compliance with Inspiration. Remember that even overturning tables and chairs in righteous anger against the "den of thieves" (Matthew 21:13) that oppressed the poor (*Experiences in Australia*, pg. 190) is not out of the question!

This interpretation squares fully with the overwhelming evidence of written inspired counsel, along with historically recorded activism, and is *not in one iota* a political polemic.

Chapter Ten:
Conclusion and Final
Discussion

We condensed a good amount of information into these pages, and so much more could be said on the topic. It is my hope with this volume to spur an interest in a greater study of the three angels' messages and its connection to social relationships and justice.

Since the Gospel Commission directs us to make

disciples of all nations for Christ, it behooves us to be able to relate to people of all cultures and walks of life.

The Christian religion knows no prejudice of any kind, except for the prejudice against sin.

Therefore, there can be no room in the Remnant Church for any racism, or elitism, or cultural and ethnical favoritism, despite the "patriotic" nationalistic rhetoric we hear so often just now. God's kingdom will be comprised of people from all earthly societies, and the everlasting Gospel is to be preached to "every nation, and kindred, and tongue, and people."

As we have seen in the previous chapters, Babylon has made the nations drunk with the wine of the wrath of her fornication. The analogy of fornication refers to the illegitimate union of church and state which Christ forbids (John 18:36).

Under Babylon, all the nations have practiced a level of injustice towards various groups and have shed the blood of innocents. James writes with no uncertainty:

> *"Your gold and silver is cankered; and the rust of them shall be a witness against you, and shall eat your flesh as it were fire... Ye have condemned and killed the just; and he doth not resist you."*

- James 5:3, 6 KJV

John the Revelator's language is no less poetic:

> *"And the ten horns which thou sawest upon the beast, these shall hate the whore, and shall make her desolate and naked, and shall eat her flesh, and burn her with fire...And he cried mightily with a strong voice, saying, Babylon the great is fallen, is fallen... For all nations have drunk of the wine of the wrath of her fornication...and the merchants of the earth are*

waxed   rich   through   the
abundance of her delicacies..."

- Revelation 17:16; 18:2-3, KJV

The Apocalyptic vision does not portray a socialist or secular power as Babylon, but rather a church-state union (represented by the fornication of the harlot, a symbol of an apostate church), enriching the nations of the world with gold, silver, a litany of valuable merchandise...along with "slaves, and souls of men" (Revelation 18:13 KJV).

It is also clear that when secular movements decry injustice, Babylon will only respond with more oppression. The Remnant are tasked with calling people out of Babylon and warning the rest of the world about the abusive practices of the Beast.

Satan has been very busy, managing to make even many among God's people call evil "good" and good "evil." Cries for justice are dismissed as "political" andeven heretical.

Alonzo T. Jones, writing for the January 18, 1900

edition of the *American Sentinel*, protested the American occupation of the Philippines. In what he termed an "act of robbery," the McKinley administration decided to "benevolently assimilate" the Philippine islands after they declared independence from Spain.

In truth, Jones laments, the American government of that day wanted to exploit the trade routes the island nation provided, and Filipino people, according to U.S. Senator Albert J. Beveridge, were

> *"not capable of self-government. How could they be? They are not of a self-governing race...They are as a people, dull and stupid, and incurably indolent."*

Incensed, A. T. Jones responded,

> *"We have heard of white people in America who were dull, stupid, and indolent, but we have never heard that for this reason*

they ought to be deprived of the
right to vote."

The early Adventists saw a need to confront prejudice. Unfortunately, as the decades went by and more and more American Adventists absorbed Southern evangelical rhetoric, they began to abandon the idea that racial minorities were disadvantaged. Many came to allege that minorities were now the oppressors, that "immigrants" were "stealing" their jobs, and that racial minorities had now acquired unfair advantages.

"Systemic racism is a myth," they declare, and offer example after example for their reasons. It is true we have advanced in leaps and bounds away from slavery and Jim Crow. But because Satan is the master at oppression and injustice, he sows seeds of doubt in people's minds...doubt that the sure word of prophecyis true.

"Slavery will again be revived in
the Southern States; for the spirit
of slavery still lives,"

declares the Messenger of God in *Manuscript Releases*, Vol. 2, page 299. This statement was written 33 years after Emancipation, and it is clear Ellen White saw that racial slavery in the South will return because its "spirit" still "lives."

Yet many, even in God's Remnant Church today, deny this will ever happen. On the contrary, they see movements for racial equality as antithetical to the Gospel, and it is a great shame, and a rejection of our classical Adventist beliefs.

Why is it hard to believe that an oppressive ideology such as racism is systemic, when we believe the corruptions of Babylon are embedded in its core system? Why is it difficult to believe that America, as blessed and as enlightened as she is, will speak (and has always been speaking to a certain extent) as a Dragon and erect an image to the Beast, and in this sense will always have ingrained in her a system of oppression since the inception of the nation? This means programmed within her system are still premises that, once revived, will spell an end to the Republic, social equality, and freedom for many.

The three angels' messages, which inform our propheticcommission as a church, clearly outline the contrast between the apostate system and the Remnant of God.

The apostate system enriches the nations through oppression, and it is our duty to cry out against the injustices we see. Christ did the same, and so should we.

> *"Woe to you, scribes and Pharisees, hypocrites! For you pay tithe of mint and anise and cummin, and have neglected the weightier matters of the law: justice and mercy and faith."*

- Matthew 23:23, NKJV

Let us make it clear. Social justice is not the totality of the Gospel, though it is certainly a part of it. As a parallel example, we know that Ellen White says that "the gospel includes health reform in all its phases" (*Medical Ministry*, p.

159), but this doesn't make health reform the whole Gospel. The Gospel is the good news of salvation provisioned to all men and women by the sacrifice of the Lamb of God. Practicing justice is only one aspect of godly living, and just as the health reform message is not the whole Gospel, but simply a portion thereof, the practice of justice and equity will allow all to see that God is just and not partial. When the people of God cry for justice on behalf of all oppressed people of the world, their witness will be the more powerful.

Inspiration tells us,

> *"I was instructed that I must ever urge upon those who profess to believe the truth, the necessity of practicing the truth...I was charged not to neglect or pass by those who were being wronged... Disagreeable though the duty may be, I am to reprove the oppressor, and plead for justice."*

- Ellen G. White, *Selected Messages*, Book 1, pg. 33.

The Remnant Church must not be afraid to stand up for those who are wronged. There are many who would even be more effective ministers of the Gospel if they would only show empathy with the plight of the oppressed.

"But I can't side with people who burn and loot buildings!" some say.

No one said you had to excuse the wrongs done in response to oppression, any more than Jesus excused the sins of the woman caught by the Pharisees committing adultery.

After he wrote on the ground and rebuked the gathered crowd, the accusers dropped their stones and left. Sister White wrote of that moment,

> *"And one by one they turned from His presence, guilty and condemned of greater sins than the poor woman whom they had thought worthy of death."*

-   Ellen G. White, *Letter 28*, 1888.

The church and its members do not need to unite with worldly organizations in the quest for Biblical justice. But neither must we be found opposing worldly groups that seek justice and equity; it is not our job or calling to oppose them, for we will be seen by them as allies of those that do oppress and abuse, damaging our vital Present Truth message.

Rather, it is our job to affirm the voices of the needy and oppressed, to lend a hand of compassion to the forsaken, and to be at the head, not the tail, of a movement—apart from the world—to end prejudice and oppression of all kinds, and to protest against the abuses and sins of Babylon by the power of the Gospel of Jesus Christ, and through the three angels' messages.

Ellet J. Waggoner of 1888 Minneapolis General Conference fame and co-editor of *The American Sentry* with A. T. Jones once wrote, two years before that famous Conference:

"If the struggle be between

Christianity and infidelity, we take the side of Christianity. If between a Christian and an infidel, we stop and inquire into the cause. If the Christian is endeavoring to deprive the infidel of his rights, we will ignore his profession and defend the infidel. True Christianity robs no one of his rights, but its followers do to others as they would that others should do to them."

- E. J. Waggoner, *The American Sentry*, January, 1886.

There is a reason why Christ's ministry was so effective; crowds flocked around Him for healing, and we have no record of Him turning anyone away. He rebuked the prejudice of the Sadducees and the Pharisees, and no doubt there were many of the poor, hungry, destitute, and the lowest rungs of society within earshot and heard His impassioned chastisements of the abuses of the religious elite.

No wonder the crowds gathered and listened to the Gospel at His feet. He was concerned with their temporal welfare and how they were treated as individuals. They then knew that in Heaven was a kingdom they could live in without being discriminated against, looked down upon, or condemned because of their social status. It was a Kingdom they wanted to live in with the God who forsook the riches of that Kingdom to be among them as a servant of servants, and the lowest of the low, despite being the King of kings. We are to reflect the mind of Christ, and as a child of the King, we must emulate the example of our Redeemer and Lord.

This is not politics, but simple Christian *charity* and *duty*.

About the Author

Lemuel Valendez Sapian is from Denton, Texas and holds a Bachelor's of Arts degree in History from the University of North Texas. Married to Michelle, together they have four fast-growing children. His passion is for world, religious, American and military historical studies. A lifelong Christian, he is a minister in the Seventh-day Adventist Church, a music composer and avid traveler.

www.lemuelsapianbooks.com